COMMON CORE

Grade 7

CLINICS

English Language Arts

Reading Literature

...on Core Clinics, English Language Arts, Reading Literature, Grade 7
.../ 372NA

...3: 978-0-7836-8483-3

...mage: © Photolink/Photolibrary

...h Learning® 136 Madison Avenue, 7th Floor, New York, NY 10016

...2 Triumph Learning, LLC
...is an imprint of Triumph Learning®

8 7 6 5

ALL ABOUT YOUR BOOK

COMMON CORE CLINICS will help you master important reading skills.

Each lesson has a **Learn About It** box that teaches the idea. A sample passage focuses on the skill. A **graphic organizer** shows you a reading strategy.

Each lesson has a **Try It** passage with **guided reading**.

HOTS Higher-Order Thinking Skills

Questions that make you think further about what you read.

Apply It provides **independent practice** for reading passages, answering short-answer questions, and responding to writing prompts.

able of Contents

Character, Setting, and Plot

Learn About It

Fiction is a literary work that is made up. A work of fiction includes particular elements. Setting, character, and plot work together to tell a story. The **setting** is *where* and *when* the story takes place. **Characters** are the people, animals, or other creatures in the story. Usually there is a **main character** around which the story's plot centers. The **plot** is the sequence of events. The plot often includes a **conflict**, or problem, and a **resolution**. Understanding how these elements interact can enhance a reader's comprehension of the text.

Read the passage. Identify how the characters, setting, and plot work together to tell a story.

Kamara stood outside the Warren Public Library on Saturday morning. She and Marnie had volunteered to knit blankets at an event for Warren Children's Hospital. But Marnie wasn't there. Had she changed her mind?

Kamara groaned at the thought as she checked the yarn in her knitting bag. Glancing up, she breathed a huge sigh of relief as she watched Marnie's car pull up.

Story Elements		
Characters	**Setting**	**Plot**
Main: Kamara **Supporting:** Marnie	**Where:** Warren Public Library **When:** Saturday morning	**Conflict:** Kamara does not know if Marnie will meet her. **Events:** Kamara stands at the library. Kamara groans and checks her knitting bag. **Resolution:** Marnie arrives.

Try It

Read the passage. Underline the words that help you identify the characters, setting, and plot, including conflict and resolution. Look for examples of how these elements interact with each other. Use the questions to help you.

Meeting Jean-Luc

I met Jean-Luc on Monday morning, when my first-period teacher naively introduced him to the class as if he were some kind of celebrity. Even Jean-Luc groaned when she asked him to join her at the head of the room, and I'm not sure he understood all that much English. I watched from the back row and tapped my pen absently on the side of the desk. I could never quite figure out why foreign exchange students volunteered to put themselves in the line of fire like this. Here stood Jean-Luc, for example, a French student with few English language skills and no friends in a strange country. Ms. O'Brien was somewhere in the process of asking us all to be nice to him when the bell rang. *Good luck*, *JL*, I thought absently as I crossed into the hall.

Not five minutes later, I rounded the bend to find Jean-Luc in my locker row.

"Hey," I said as I passed by, but I didn't make eye contact. I noticed that Jean-Luc was having trouble with the locker combination, and speaking unintelligible French phrases every few moments as a result. Finally, he kicked the locker and shouted something at it.

"Whoa," I said as I glanced around the hall. "Take it easy there, JL. Let me give it a shot for you."

Jean-Luc stared at me for a moment while I gestured stupidly for the piece of paper with the combination on it. Finally, he handed it over. I must have embarrassed him when I got it open on the first try, because his already pink face turned a darker shade of red.

"Piece of cake," I said casually as I handed him the combination code. Then I tapped him on the shoulder and walked down the hall to math class.

When the second-period bell rang, I was amused to find JL walking through the door. Glancing around the room, he saw me and tentatively headed over to the empty desk on my right.

> As you read, consider how the setting of the story might make Jean-Luc feel a little nervous.

> How does the narrator react to Jean-Luc's problem at the locker? What does this suggest about the narrator?

Continued on the next page ➤

Continued from the previous page

"Are you following me?" I asked in mock seriousness when he sat down, but the joke went unnoticed as he gave me a blank stare. Sighing, I opened my book to the day's math lesson.

And so it happened that as the day progressed, and I moved from class to class, JL was somehow always there. By the time I hit sixth period, I was outright laughing. I think JL's mood was improving, too. He started to smile when he saw me, and even tried to make conversation once or twice.

By the end of the day, I not-so-surprisingly met JL at the lockers. He looked exhausted from his experience today. "So, how was your first day?" I asked as I turned the dial on my locker. I glanced up to find him staring up at the ceiling, as if trying to remember something.

"It's like you say," he said in broken English, "a piece of cake."

Laughing, I nodded my head and said, "That's the spirit, JL. Until tomorrow."

Jean-Luc smiled back and said, "Until tomorrow, Dave."

My last thought as I walked down the hall was that at some point during the day JL had paid enough attention to learn my name. Maybe there was hope for him yet.

In what ways does the narrator show humor throughout the series of events that occur?

Think about how both Jean-Luc and the narrator change from the beginning of the school day to the end.

HOTS Analyze

Suppose the narrator and Jean-Luc did not have the same classes. How might that have affected the story's plot? Explain the importance of the setting to the passage.

Apply It

Read the passage. Ask yourself questions about the elements of character, setting, and plot, and how they interact in this story. Answer the questions that follow.

Pecos Bill and Widow-Maker

Pecos Bill chose the company of people over the coyote family he grew up with, but he wasn't always happy with his decision. Human company was usually tolerable and the food was sure better, but the yakking was hard to get used to. It seemed that people just loved to yak, yak, yak, all day and all night, and he found it was often best to ignore it. One day though, while sitting around a campfire, Bill heard something that made him almost come out of his boots.

"I think that wild stallion was breathing smoke and fire," one of the cowboys whispered excitedly. "He gallops at the speed of light, and can stop a cyclone in its tracks. We'll never be able to catch him."

"I'm givin' up," grunted another one. "We've been in his dust for a week now. There ain't no way we're gonna' get a hold of him. That Widow-Maker's just playin' games with us, boys. You know it's a losin' battle. They don't call him Widow-Maker for nothing!"

"Uh, pardon me for interrupting," said Pecos Bill, "but do y'all happen to know where this Widow-Maker is? Sounds like he and I are kindred spirits, if y'know what I mean."

The cowboys pointed to the Powder River, and that's when Pecos got his first glance of Widow-Maker. The brown stallion galloped across the horizon, his feet barely touching the ground. Pecos knew at once that he was meant to ride the stallion, and so he ran like the wind to catch up to him.

Widow-Maker snorted at the idea of a man trying to catch him on foot, but he soon saw that Pecos was no ordinary man. For four nights and three days the man ran after the horse, all around North America, from Mexico to Canada and back, and twice around the state of Texas.

Although he barely broke a sweat, Widow-Maker was getting tired of the game and decided to teach Pecos a lesson. He neighed and rose up high above Pecos with the intent to scare him away. But before the stallion knew what was happening, Pecos had leaped into the air, twisting and landing square on Widow-Maker's back.

Widow-Maker didn't like this surprise one bit, so he tried to throw him off, bucking and bolting in all directions. In less than twenty seconds, he had covered two miles. But Pecos Bill stayed on his back like the true cowboy he was. Then Widow-Maker scraped and threw Pecos Bill against every tree and rock in Texas, until Pecos was torn up and bleeding, but still he held on.

Continued on the next page ➤

Continued from the previous page

When Widow-Maker finally took a moment to rest, Pecos stroked his neck and spoke to him in the language of the animals. He told Widow-Maker that there was nothing to fear and that they would be great friends with many adventures ahead of them. Widow-Maker considered this and thought it might not be so bad to have Pecos Bill on his back, after all. He decided to befriend the man, and their many adventures are still talked about today.

Answer these questions about "Pecos Bill and Widow-Maker." Write your answers in complete sentences.

1. How is the campfire setting important to the story's plot?

_____

_____

2. How can you describe the relationship between the characters?

_____

_____

3. How does Pecos Bill solve his problem?

_____

_____

4. Why is it important that Pecos Bill rides Widow-Maker around North America?

_____

_____

5. How does the setting of the Old West help the reader understand Pecos Bill's character?

_____

_____

Theme

Learn About It

> The **theme** of a story is its central message or lesson. It is usually a general statement about life, such as "Be kind to those in need" or "Appearances can be deceiving." The theme may be directly stated, but it often must be inferred based on the details and events in the story.

Read the passage and identify the theme. Think about how the details of the passage help you determine the story's lesson.

adapted from

The Oak and the Reeds
by Aesop

A very large oak was uprooted by the wind and thrown across a stream. It fell among some reeds, which it thus addressed: "I wonder how you, who are so light and weak, are not entirely crushed by these strong winds."

They replied, "You fight and contend with the wind, and consequently you are destroyed; while we on the contrary bend before the least breath of air, and therefore remain unbroken, and escape."

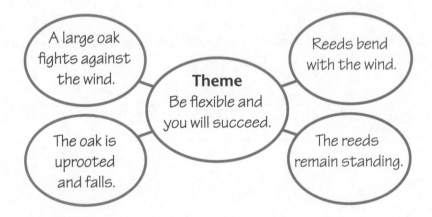

Try It

Read the passage. Identify the theme. Then go back and underline the details in the passage that helped you figure out the message or lesson. Use the questions to help you.

Choice Anxiety

Plink-plink-plink.

Jason opened an eye, tensing instinctively in the darkness of the room. Glancing at the alarm clock, he saw that it was 3:00 in the morning.

Plink-plink-plink.

This time, Jason raised his head from the pillow. The sound was coming from his bedroom window, and he had a feeling he knew just what it was.

Climbing out of bed, he shuffled over to the window and unlocked it before pulling it open. The cool night air blew into the room, sending a shiver through his body.

"Jason!" a voice whispered loudly from below.

"Molly?" Jason asked sleepily. "What are you doing?"

He stared down at his best friend, Molly Lin, who was pacing restlessly in his front yard. Frowning, he closed the window and tiptoed down the hall past his parents' bedroom. Making his way down the stairs, he asked himself why he was even surprised to find her throwing pebbles at his window in the middle of the night. Molly had a way of doing things that were completely unexpected.

Making his way out the front door, he spun around and almost crashed into his very excited friend.

"Mol, what are you doing?" he asked, hiding his annoyance. "It's the middle of the night!"

"I couldn't wait to tell you," she replied with a huge grin, still whispering. "I've made a monumental decision, and I wanted you to be the first to know!"

Jason held his breath, waiting to hear the latest crazy scheme that Molly had concocted.

"I'm running for class president!" she shouted, before quickly covering her mouth as a neighbor's dog started barking.

> How do you know Jason and Molly are close friends?

> Think about why Molly chose to tell Jason *first* about her decision.

Continued on the next page ➤

Continued from the previous page

Jason stared at Molly for a moment, blinking stupidly as he tried to think of something to say. This was, in fact, huge news . . . and not in a good way. Jason's team captain on the football team, Ryan, was going to run for class president. Jason knew that Ryan would be counting on his support.

"Well? Isn't this exciting news?" Molly asked a little uncertainly. "I thought you'd be a little more responsive. Are you still sleeping?" she teased.

"No, no, that's great, Mol," Jason finally replied. "I think you'd make a great class president." The truth of the matter was that *both* Ryan and Molly would be great class leaders.

"So, I was hoping that you could come to see my announcement tomorrow," Molly continued. "Maybe you could cheer me on . . . you might be the only one, after all." Molly knew that Ryan was her competition, and he was very popular. Jason couldn't help but admire her bravery for taking on such a daunting task. She was definitely the underdog. It reminded him of all the other crazy things that Molly had dragged him into over the years . . . things that he would have never done himself. Yet, those were some of the best times he'd ever had.

Chuckling, Jason shook his head as he realized that his choice was an easy one to make. "Of course I'll be there," he said. "I can't think of anywhere else I'd rather be."

Identify the conflict that Jason has in the story. What decision does he have to make?

Think about how Jason's decision helps to define the friendship between him and Molly.

HOTS Analyze

What is the overall message in the story? How does the theme of the passage reflect Jason's actions?

Apply It

Read the passage. Determine the story's theme, based on the text. Circle the details that support that lesson. Answer the questions that follow.

The Daydreamer
an Indian folktale

There once was an oil man who sold pots of oil at the local market every weekend. He would carry the oil in a basket that he balanced on his head. This week, the man had too many oil pots to carry, so he took another basket and asked a man to help him for a wage of two coins. The second man agreed readily, for he had not worked in many days. Although this man lived a small existence, he had great dreams.

As the second man balanced his basket of oil pots on his head, the pair set off down the dirt path. The oil man took care to walk carefully and to maintain his balance as he traveled, for he knew that the oil was his livelihood and it was important that it did not spill.

The second man, however, was not as careful as the first. Instead of paying attention to his oil pots, his thoughts began to wander to the two coins he would earn for the task.

I will buy a meal with the first coin, thought the man excitedly. *With the second coin, I will gain some chickens. These chickens will grow and multiply, and I will soon have eggs. I can then sell the eggs to buy some goats!*

As the second man walked along the dirt path, he began to imagine his very own herd of goats. *I can then sell some goats to buy cows, and as the cows breed, I can sell those, as well! Soon I will have enough money to buy my own land . . . and I will marry . . . and have my own family . . . who will help me in the fields . . . and the land will give me everything I need!*

"Watch out!" shouted the oil man from somewhere at the edge of the man's daydream. Before he could avoid it, the second man tripped over a large rock in front of him on the dirt path. Stumbling, he managed to catch himself before falling, but the basket on his head tipped and crashed loudly to the ground. In agony, the second man watched not only the oil, but also his dreams, seep into the thirsty earth.

The oil man turned in anger to the second man. "You fool!" he shouted. "You have destroyed half of my income for the day. Do you have any idea what you have done to me?"

Continued on the next page ➡

Continued from the previous page

"Not nearly so much as I have done to myself," the second man replied in despair. "I have destroyed a day's income for you, but a lifetime of income for myself."

The oil man carefully studied the second man's face and decided that, although the man spoke in riddles, he spoke the truth. The oil man realized that this man's disappointment was much greater than his own, so he chose not to request that the man pay him back. Instead, the oil man sent the second man on his way, as he no longer needed his help. The second man dragged his heavy feet along the path as he walked with a sad heart back from where he came.

Answer these questions about "The Daydreamer." Write your answers in complete sentences.

1. How does the oil man show that hard work is rewarding?

_____

_____

2. Why is the story called "The Daydreamer"?

_____

_____

3. What lesson does the second man learn in the story?

_____

_____

4. What is the theme of the story?

_____

_____

_____

_____

Summarize Text

Learn About It

To **summarize** is to briefly restate the general idea of something. A summary of a story includes only the *most important details* relevant to the *characters* and *plot*. Any unrelated details, examples, or explanations in the text should be excluded from a summary.

Look for the most important details in the passage. These details will help you summarize the text.

Abigail was inspired by her favorite song on the ride home from school.

"That's it!" she shouted in triumphant glee. "I'll make my very own radio for the science fair coming up next month."

As her mother slowed for a red light, Abigail's logical mind began to piece together the different materials she needed for the project. Excitedly, she turned to her mother in the front seat.

"Can we stop at the hardware store on the way home?" she asked with a sparkle in her eye.

Detail	Detail	Detail
Abigail is inspired to make a radio for the science fair.	She thinks of all the materials she will need to make the radio.	She asks her mother to stop at a hardware store for the materials.

Summary

Abigail is inspired to build a radio for the science fair. She asks her mother to take her to the hardware store to buy some supplies.

Try It

Read the passage. Look for important details that relate to the story's main ideas and key points. Underline these details and use them to help you summarize the text. Use the questions to help you.

The Scotland Blues

The solid stone bridge stretched endlessly before the four weary travelers in yellow raincoats. The Gallaghers had left their miniature rental car in the parking lot nearby, and now they slowly began to make their way over the bridge toward the Eilean Donan Castle. Chris tilted his head back to view the top of this famous Scottish structure, only to feel the cold reality of a wet raindrop on his face.

"Ack! It's raining *again*!" he shouted to no one in particular.

There was a collective groan from the rest of the family, as everyone picked up their pace to get inside the castle.

The Gallaghers' vacation to Scotland had seemed like a good idea when they planned it. Chris was fascinated by anything related to the Scottish Highlands, and Pete loved the outdoors. Mom and Dad just wanted to go someplace where they could speak English, so everyone had agreed on Scotland surprisingly quickly. The plane ride was fairly uneventful, as well. But once the family touched down in Edinburgh, things started to go downhill.

> **Which details on this page relate to the main ideas and key points of the story? Which details are unnecessary?**

> **Summarize what happens in the first four paragraphs of the story.**

Continued on the next page ➤

Continued from the previous page

For one thing, the weather had not been cooperating all week—rain, rain, and more rain. It was in the forecast on a daily basis—day and night—and not just in the capital city of Edinburgh. The family members had finally rented a car to drive up into the Highlands in an attempt to escape the weather, but the stubborn rain was apparently intent on following them and ruining their trip.

> **Review the information in the seventh paragraph. Give a summary of this information in one sentence.**

For another thing, the normal tourist spots all seemed to be very difficult to find, closed for renovations, or both. Dad had more than once muttered the phrase "wild goose chase" while trying to figure out directions to a hidden castle or abbey. As a result, the family had spent much of the vacation driving in circles . . . in a small car . . . in the rain.

So it was with understandably heavy hearts that the Gallaghers now entered the Eilean Donan Castle. But a funny thing happened while they toured the interior of the structure. In what seemed like the blink of an eye, the clouds parted and revealed a bright welcoming sun. The grass around the castle seemed greener, and the water in the surrounding loch sparkled a brilliant blue. Scotland transformed from a gray, dreary world to quite a magical place. It was a stunning change, and when the Gallaghers exited the castle, they found themselves overwhelmed by it.

> **Which parts of the eighth through eleventh paragraphs belong in a summary of the text?**

Chris turned to his brother with a look of disbelief, while Mom raised her face and closed her eyes, enjoying (at last) the warmth of the sun. Dad paused for just a moment before he began sprinting wildly across the bridge toward the car park.

"Dad! Where are you going?" shouted Chris.

"Come on!" he shouted over his shoulder as he ran. "If we hurry, we can get to Inverness today and maybe see the Loch Ness Monster!"

Chris and Pete glanced quickly at their mother, and they all shared a relieved smile before racing toward the little rental car.

HOTS Understand

Summarize the Gallaghers' vacation in Scotland. Use details about the characters and their actions from the story to support your summary.

Apply It

Read the passage. Underline details that relate to the main ideas in the text. Circle the most important of these details to restate in a summary. Answer the questions that follow.

excerpted and adapted from

White Fang

by Jack London

Down the frozen waterway toiled a string of wolfish dogs. Their breath froze in the air as it left their mouths, spouting forth as vapor that settled upon the hair of their bodies and formed into crystals of frost. The dogs were in a leather harness, and leather traces attached them to a sled which dragged along behind.

In advance of the dogs, on wide snowshoes, toiled a man. At the rear of the sled toiled a second man. Their bodies were covered with fur and soft-tanned leather. Eyelashes and cheeks and lips were so coated with the crystals from their frozen breath that their faces were not discernible.

An hour went by, and a second hour. The pale light of the short sunless day was beginning to fade, when a faint far cry arose on the still air. It might have been a lost soul wailing, had it not been invested with a certain sad fierceness and hungry eagerness. The front man turned his head until his eyes met the eyes of the man behind.

A second cry arose, piercing the silence with needle-like shrillness. Both men located the sound. It was to the rear, somewhere in the snowy expanse they had just traversed. A third and answering cry arose, also to the rear and to the left of the second cry.

"They're after us, Bill," said the man at the front.

"Meat is scarce," answered his comrade. "I ain't seen a rabbit sign for days."

At the fall of darkness they swung the dogs into a cluster of spruce trees on the edge of the waterway and made a camp. The wolf-dogs, clustered on the far side of the fire, snarled and bickered among themselves, but were not inclined to stray off into the darkness.

"Henry," said his companion, munching with deliberation the beans he was eating, "did you happen to notice the way them dogs kicked up when I was a-feedin' 'em?"

"They did cut up more'n usual," Henry acknowledged.

Continued on the next page ➤

Continued from the previous page

"How many dogs 've we got, Henry?"

"Six."

"Well, Henry . . ." Bill stopped for a moment, in order that his words might gain greater significance. "I took six fish out of the bag. I gave one fish to each dog, an', Henry, I was one fish short."

"You counted wrong."

"We've got six dogs," the other reiterated dispassionately. "I took out six fish. One didn't get any fish. I came back to the bag afterward an' got 'm his fish."

"Henry," Bill went on. "I won't say they was all dogs, but there was seven of 'm that got fish."

Henry stopped eating to glance across the fire and count the dogs.

"I saw the other one run off across the snow," Bill announced with cool positiveness. "I saw seven."

Henry did not reply, but munched on in silence, until, the meal finished, he topped it with a final cup of coffee. He wiped his mouth with the back of his hand and said:

"Then you're thinkin' it was—"

A long wailing cry, fiercely sad, from somewhere in the darkness, had interrupted him. He stopped to listen to it, then he finished his sentence with a wave of his hand toward the sound of the cry, "—one of them?"

Answer these questions about the excerpt from "White Fang." Write your answers in complete sentences.

1. Write one sentence that summarizes the first six paragraphs of the passage.

_____

_____

2. Give a short summary of what Henry learns during his conversation with Bill.

_____

_____

3. Summarize how Bill knows that seven animals ate the fish.

_____

_____

_____

_____

4. Write a summary of the important events in the passage.

_____

_____

_____

_____

Drawing and Supporting Inference

Learn About It

An **inference** is an educated guess. Readers use **textual details** or clues and their own **prior knowledge** to draw inferences in a literary text. Readers make many inferences as they read. These inferences help them comprehend the text and make connections between ideas. Inferences should always be supported by details in the text.

Use the details in the text to help you make inferences about the main character. Think about how these inferences help you understand the character and the story.

Renee sat very still in her father's van.

"Are you ready?" he asked with a reassuring smile.

"Sure," she replied nonchalantly, but inside her stomach was churning, and she felt like she wanted to flee and hide.

Renee's father opened the van's back doors and pressed a button to activate the ramp. Students gave her curious looks as they passed by, but many others didn't seem to notice, and some even gave her a quick smile. Renee took a deep breath and held her head high. "Here goes nothing," she whispered, as she wheeled herself toward the school's main door.

Text Clues	Prior Knowledge	Inference
Renee's stomach is churning. Renee feels like she wants to run and hide.	Feeling nervous can upset your stomach. Feeling nervous can make you want to escape a situation.	Renee feels nervous.

(+ between Text Clues and Prior Knowledge; arrow → between Prior Knowledge and Inference)

Try It

Read the excerpt about a man named Ogilvy who goes to examine what appears to be a meteorite that has crashed into Earth. Look for clues that help you make inferences about the events and characters in the excerpt. Circle the details that best support the inferences you make. Use the questions to help you.

excerpted and adapted from

The War of the Worlds
by H.G. Wells

Then suddenly Ogilvy noticed with a start that some of the ashy incrustation that covered the meteorite was falling off the circular edge of the end. It was dropping off in flakes and raining down upon the sand. A large piece suddenly came off and fell with a sharp noise that brought his heart into his mouth.

And then he perceived that, very slowly, the circular top of the cylinder was rotating on its body. It was such a gradual movement that he discovered it only through noticing that a black mark that had been near him five minutes ago was now at the other side of the circumference. Even then he scarcely understood what this indicated, until he heard a muffled grating sound and saw the black mark jerk forward an inch or so. Then the thing came upon him in a flash. The cylinder was artificial—hollow—with an end that screwed out! Something within the cylinder was unscrewing the top!

> How does Ogilvy feel when the ash begins to fall from the cylinder in the first paragraph? How do you know he feels this way?

"Good heavens!" said Ogilvy. "There's a man in it—men in it! Half roasted to death! Trying to escape!"

The thought of the confined creature was so dreadful to him that he forgot the heat and went forward to the cylinder to help turn. But luckily the dull radiation arrested him before he could burn his hands on the still-glowing metal. At that he stood irresolute for a moment, then turned, scrambled out of the pit, and set off running

Continued on the next page ▶

Continued from the previous page

wildly into Woking. The time then must have been somewhere about six o'clock. He met a wagoner and tried to make him understand, but the tale he told and his appearance were so wild—his hat had fallen off in the pit—that the man simply drove on. He was equally unsuccessful with the potman who was just unlocking the doors of the public-house by Horsell Bridge. The fellow thought he was a lunatic at large and made an unsuccessful attempt to shut him into the taproom. That sobered him a little; and when he saw Henderson, the London journalist, in his garden, he called over the palings and made himself understood.

Think about how the wagoner in the fourth paragraph must have felt when he saw Ogilvy. Look for details to support this inference.

"Henderson," he called, "you saw that shooting star last night?"

"Well?" said Henderson.

"It's out on Horsell Common now. But it's something more than a meteorite. It's a cylinder—an artificial cylinder, man! And there's something inside."

Ogilvy told him all that he had seen. Henderson was a minute or so taking it in. Then he dropped his spade, snatched up his jacket, and came out into the road. The two men hurried back at once to the common, and found the cylinder still lying in the same position. But now the sounds inside had ceased, and a thin circle of bright metal showed between the top and the body of the cylinder. Air was either entering or escaping at the rim with a thin, sizzling sound.

Review the eighth paragraph. What does Henderson's reaction to Ogilvy's story suggest about him?

They listened, rapped on the scaly burnt metal with a stick, and, meeting with no response, they both concluded the man or men inside must be insensible or dead.

HOTS Analyze

How do you think Ogilvy feels about the cylinder, once he sees that the lid is opening? Explain why you think he feels this way using details from the passage.

Apply It

Read the passage. Circle the details that help you make inferences. Write any prior knowledge you use next to the details. Answer the questions that follow.

Sunday Tea

"Hello, Maga," I announce as my grandmother opens the door. Her eyes light up when she sees me. They always do.

"Alyssa, my beautiful girl," she replies lovingly as she places a hand on my cheek. "Your mother?"

"Parking the car," I answer. It is the same greeting that we have shared every Sunday for the past ten years. I take comfort in it, just as I do in seeing the sparkle in Maga's eyes and the curl in her perfectly coiffed hair.

As I step inside, I see that she has laid out a tray of my favorite cookies with my favorite china tea set. I follow as she leads the way into the living room and pours me some tea. From somewhere in my subconscious, I realize that chamomile will always remind me of Maga, even many years from now when I am much older and she is gone. I close my eyes and let the scent waft slowly up to my nostrils. Holding the cup in both hands, I welcome the emotions it stirs. The feel of the china is so comforting that it makes me laugh.

I glance up to find her staring at me, like she always does. I wonder how she can find me so interesting and special when most days I wish I were someone else. Seeing the pride in her eyes makes me feel stronger . . . and oddly happy.

"Hi, Mom!" my mother shouts as she bounds through the door. She is holding a large three-ringed binder in the crook of her arm.

Continued on the next page ➤

Continued from the previous page

"We have a surprise for you, Maga," I say mysteriously. This time, I have the sparkle in my eye. "Guess what Uncle Bruce found in his attic this week?"

"What is it?" she asks uncertainly. "Is that . . . Papa's photo album?" Her normal expression is replaced with something different and nostalgic, and Mom winks at me as she hurries over to flop on the sofa with the book.

Together, the three of us eat cookies and drink tea and look at photos. I listen as Maga tells me about her brother and the wars he fought in as an Air Force pilot. I look at pictures of Maga when she was my age, and I wonder if we would have been friends. I see my great-grandmother and great-uncle and great-aunt, and I laugh when Maga says that I am like her sister—because I love adventure—and I am like her brother—because I am loyal. Mom asks Maga questions, but I don't hear them. I am mesmerized by the scenes before me, and drawn to the strangers to whom I am so deeply connected.

As I pour myself more tea, Maga leans in to tell me how lucky she is to have me here with her. I don't tell her that I am the lucky one because I fear it will sound silly . . . but I feel it deep within me, and I know without a doubt that it is true.

Answer these questions about "Sunday Tea." Write your answers in complete sentences.

1. Why does Alyssa enjoy the smell of chamomile so much?

_____

_____

2. Which details in the fifth paragraph provide insight into Alyssa's personality?

_____

_____

3. Why does Alyssa have a sparkle in her eye in the seventh paragraph?

_____

_____

4. Which details support the inference that Alyssa cares about her family's history?

_____

_____

5. What type of relationship does Alyssa have with her grandmother? Explain how you know.

_____

_____

_____

_____

Supporting an Analysis of Text

Learn About It

A reader **analyzes** different ideas in a story as part of comprehending what he or she reads. Some of these ideas are directly stated in the text, and sometimes the reader makes **inferences** about the text when analyzing it. Regardless of the type of analysis, it should be supported by specific **details** in the text. A reader should always be able to provide textual evidence to justify his or her analysis.

Read the passage. Analyze the main character's problem, and then find details in the text that support your analysis.

Roberto's mother bumped into him as he exited his bedroom in his soccer uniform. His face looked tired and anxious.

"I thought that practice was tomorrow, Roberto," said his mother in a concerned voice.

"No, Mama," he replied. "Tomorrow is the play rehearsal and band practice. I don't know when I will find time for the science project due on Friday."

"We will need to discuss this later," his mother replied. "I do not want your grades to start slipping!"

Analysis
Roberto has too many extracurricular activities.

Text Evidence	**Text Evidence**	**Text Evidence**
Roberto's face shows that he is tired and anxious.	Roberto cannot find time to work on his science project.	Roberto's mother is concerned about Roberto's grades.

Try It

Read this passage about Jane, an orphan who must live with her cruel aunt, Mrs. Reed. Underline the words that help you understand Jane's experience. Use the questions to help you.

excerpted and adapted from

Jane Eyre

by Charlotte Brontë

There was no possibility of taking a walk that day. We had been wandering, indeed, in the leafless shrubbery an hour in the morning; but since dinner, the cold winter wind had brought with it clouds so somber, and a rain so penetrating, that further outdoor exercise was now out of the question.

I was glad of it: I never liked long walks, especially on chilly afternoons: dreadful to me was the coming home in the raw twilight, with nipped fingers and toes, and a heart saddened by the chidings of Bessie, the nurse, and humbled by my physical inferiority to Eliza, John, and Georgiana Reed.

Eliza, John, and Georgiana were now clustered round their mamma in the drawing-room; she lay reclined on the sofa by the fireside, and with her darlings about her (for the time neither quarreling nor crying) looked perfectly happy. Me, she had dispensed from joining the group; saying 'She regretted to be under the necessity of keeping me at a distance; but that until she heard from Bessie and could discover by her own observation that I was more sociable and friendly, she really must exclude me from privileges intended only for contented, happy little children.'

"What does Bessie say I have done?" I asked.

"Jane, I don't like questions: besides, there is something truly forbidding in a child taking up her elders in that manner. Be seated somewhere, and until you can speak pleasantly, remain silent."

> Which text in the second paragraph supports the analysis that Jane is not happy where she is?

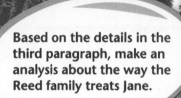

> Based on the details in the third paragraph, make an analysis about the way the Reed family treats Jane.

Continued on the next page ➤

A small breakfast-room adjoined the drawing-room.
I slipped in there. It contained a bookcase: I soon possessed
myself of a volume, taking care that it should be one stored
with pictures. I mounted into the window seat: gathering up
my feet, I sat cross-legged; and, having drawn the red curtain
nearly closed, I was shrined in double retirement.

Folds of scarlet drapery shut in my view to the right hand;
to the left were the clear panes of glass protecting, but not separating me from the drear
November day. At intervals, while turning over the leaves of my book, I studied the
aspect of that winter afternoon. Afar, it offered a pale blank of mist and cloud; near, a
scene of wet lawn and storm-beat shrub, with ceaseless rain sweeping
away wildly before a long and lamentable blast.

I returned to my book—Bewick's *History of British
Birds* . . . Each picture told a story; mysterious often to my
undeveloped understanding and imperfect feelings, yet
ever profoundly interesting: as interesting as the tales Bessie
sometimes narrated on winter evenings, when she chanced to be
in good humor, and when, having brought her ironing-table to the nursery-hearth, she
allowed us to sit about it, and while she got up Mrs. Reed's lace frills, and crimped her
night-cap borders, fed our eager attention with passages of love and adventure taken
from old fairy tales.

With Bewick on my knee, I was then happy: happy at least in my way. I feared
nothing but interruption and that came too soon. The breakfast-room door opened.

Look for text that indica
Jane is a thoughtful and
imaginative child.

Which details in the
passage suggest that Ja
is happy to be alone?

HOTS Analyze

Which details in the passage support the analysis that Jane uses
stories to escape her world? Explain how they support this idea.

Apply It

Read the passage. As you read, underline details in the text that may be useful later in an analysis of the story's characters and events. Answer the questions that follow.

The Wedding Ring

I was thirteen years old when my sister, Corinne, got married. Corinne and I were very close, despite the fact that she's six years older than me. She had always been there for me, through thick and thin, and we were best friends in our own sisterly way. So it was understandably a little unsettling when I found out that she was getting married and leaving home. Well, maybe *unsettling* isn't the best word, but rather, *traumatic*. It definitely took some time for me to get used to the idea.

The months before the wedding were a whirlwind of activity. Corinne had to attend dress fittings, plan the ceremony, make arrangements for out-of-town guests, choose the flower arrangements, etc., etc. The list went on and on, and every time I asked her to do any of the things that we always did together—play basketball in the driveway, go hiking at the park, catch a movie at the mall—she was always too busy.

"Your sister is going through a very exciting time right now, Jeannie," my mother would remind me (over and over again). "It's important that you support her and show her that you love her. Don't worry; things will go back to normal after she settles into her new life."

Continued on the next page ➤

Continued from the previous page

But how could things go back to normal when Corinne was moving away? Granted it was only a few miles, but she wouldn't be living with me anymore. It seemed that my whole world was changing and nobody noticed.

The day of the wedding could best be described as a festive extension of the months that preceded it. Corinne laughed and danced with her guests on the brightly-lit dance floor, as I weaved farther and farther away to the edge of the ballroom. Finally, I found a distant seat where I could be alone. I watched heavily as my family and Corinne's closest friends formed a small circle with Corinne by joining hands. She laughed and allowed herself to be pulled along when the circle began to move.

"Wait!" Corinne suddenly shouted above the pounding of the music and the laughter of the crowd. "Jeannie! Where's Jeannie?"

Corinne broke from the ring of hands and lifted the hem of her gown as she turned in all directions, searching the ballroom for me. Hesitantly, I stood up from my hiding place in the corner of the room. She had remembered me! The veil of sadness that had covered me for months suddenly and magically lifted. Corinne's simple gesture seemed strangely symbolic of things to come in this uncertain future between us, and I felt deeply reassured that everything would be all right.

Corinne made eye contact with me, and it was as if she could read my mind. Trotting over, she grabbed me to her and then grasped my hands. "Jeannie! Don't you disappear on me!" she shouted over the music. "I need you, sis." With that, she tightly held my hand as together we joined the wedding ring.

Answer these questions about "The Wedding Ring." Write your answers in complete sentences.

1. Which text at the beginning of the passage supports the analysis that Jeannie will miss her sister, Corinne?

_____

_____

2. What does the conversation between Jeannie and her mother suggest about her mother?

_____

_____

3. Use details from the passage to explain why Jeannie thinks the wedding is like an extension of the months that came before it.

_____

_____

4. Which details at the end of the passage support an analysis that Jeannie feels better about the future?

_____

_____

_____

_____

6 Figurative and Connotative Meanings

Learn About It

> **Figurative language** does not mean exactly what it says. The figurative meaning of a word or phrase is associated with the image that the text creates in the reader's mind. A **simile** makes a comparison using *like* or *as*. A **metaphor** makes a comparison in imaginative ways without using *like* or *as*. **Imagery** appeals to any of the five senses. **Personification** gives human qualities to nonhuman things. A word can also have a **connotative meaning** which relates to the emotions and feelings that it evokes.

Read the passage. As you read, look for language that has a figurative or connotative meaning.

Tía Lucia shouted gleefully as the car rolled up to yet another antique shop on Route 4. The shop called out to her. A crystal chandelier sparkled over a dark brown wooden coffee table. Miguel returned her look with an overly bright smile and a well-concealed moan.

Two hours and four antique shops ago, he had decided to take this ill-fated trip with her. Now, he watched as Tía Lucia exited the car and headed like a freight train toward the fifth shop.

Sighing, he stepped out to follow her. His feet were two lead blocks that required every ounce of his energy to lift. Taking a deep breath, he straightened up and opened the store door.

Types of Figurative Language	
Simile	Tía Lucia . . . headed like a freight train toward the fifth shop.
Metaphor	His feet were two lead blocks . . .
Imagery	A crystal chandelier sparkled over a dark brown wooden coffee table.
Personification	The shop called out to her.

Try It

Read the poem. Underline any words or phrases that have figurative or connotative meanings. Use the questions to help you.

excerpted and adapted from

The Two Children

by Emily Brontë

Heavy hangs the rain-drop
From the burdened spray;
Heavy broods the damp mist
On uplands far away.

> **How does the imagery of the first few lines establish the tone of the poem?**

5 Heavy looms the dull sky,
Heavy rolls the sea;
And heavy throbs the young heart
Beneath that lonely tree.

Never has a blue streak
10 Cleft the clouds since morn;
Never has his grim fate
Smiled since he was born.

Frowning on the infant,
Shadowing childhood's joy
15 Guardian-angel knows not
That melancholy boy.

Continued on the next page ➤

Continued from the previous page

Day is passing swiftly
Its sad and somber prime;
Boyhood sad is merging
20 In sadder manhood's time:

All the flowers are begging
For sun, before they close,
And he begs too—unconscious—
That sunless human rose.

25 Blossom—that the west-wind
Has never wooed to blow,
Scentless are your petals,
Your dew is cold as snow!

Child of delight, with sun-bright hair,
30 And sea-blue, sea-deep eyes!
Spirit of bliss! What brings you here
Beneath these sullen skies?

You should live in eternal spring,
Where endless day is never dim;
35 Why, Seraph, has your erring wing
Wafted thee down to weep with him?

"I—the image of light and gladness—
Saw and pitied that mournful boy,
And I vowed—if need were—to share his sadness,
40 And give to him my sunny joy.

"Guardian-angel he lacks no longer;
Evil fortune he need not fear:
Fate is strong, but love is stronger;
And *my* love is truer than angel-care."

The speaker refers to the child as a "sunless human rose." Is this a metaphor or a simile?

What comparison does the simile in line 28 make?

How is gladness personified in the poem?

Does the poet use figurative language effectively to relay the imagery to the reader? Identify three examples of figurative language in the poem that you found most effective.

Apply It

Read the passage. Circle the figurative and connotative words. Write their meanings in the margin. Answer the questions that follow.

The Tree House on Wildwood

Jamie stared up at the weathered tree house in the backyard of 247 Wildwood Road. These were her old stomping grounds. It had been almost four years since she and her family had moved away, but it might as well have been a hundred. So much had changed in Jamie's life, and her days at Wildwood had become a distant memory that most times remained in the far corners of her subconscious. But not the tree house.

Of all the things for which Jamie held a soft spot in her heart, the tree house was perhaps the dearest. Standing at the corner of Wildwood and Patterson, Jamie stared up at the wooden structure. It rose majestically before her, like a sentinel that watched over the yard to which it was assigned. Its white walls had been repainted so that they were a bright red, and the window shutters had changed from pink to black. The ladder was a strong, wooden one, instead of the one she had which was made of thick, strong ropWe. It had been so exciting to climb that ladder and crawl into the little room with the fluffy rug and old, smooth writing desk. She would always pull the ladder up behind her, effectively closing herself in her own little world.

Jamie smiled when she remembered the tea parties, journal writing, and star gazing she had done from her perch high above the yard. There were many nights that she had fallen asleep up there in her sleeping bag, only to hear her mother calling softly to her from below.

Yes, the tree house had been a good friend to Jamie; it had comforted her with its solid walls and cheery windows. It had whispered secrets to her as it creaked and moaned in the wind, and she in turn had shared with it her greatest fears and desires—at least those that were most important to a ten-year-old girl.

Continued on the next page ▶

Continued from the previous page

Suddenly, Jamie's memories were interrupted when she saw a movement from within the tree house. A boy, no older than seven or eight, poked his head through one of the side windows. He wore a red-and-white pirate's scarf on his head and a black cloth eye patch over his left eye. A long, thin stick hung limply in his right arm, but Jamie imagined that the pirate was ready to use his makeshift sword at a moment's notice.

Chuckling, she walked down the sidewalk of Wildwood, directly under the great oak tree that held this boy's pirate ship. It seemed that some things never changed, and time marched on regardless of her memories. She had deserted the tree house when she moved, so why shouldn't she expect it to find a new friend? She was oddly pleased to know that it was not lonely without her, and that a boy now had the opportunity to love it the way that she had.

Answer these questions about "The Tree House on Wildwood." Write your answers in complete sentences.

1. In the second paragraph, the author writes, "Of all the things for which Jamie held a soft spot in her heart, the tree house was perhaps the dearest." What does the phrase *soft spot* mean in this sentence?

_____

_____

2. Why does the narrator compare the tree house to a sentinel in the second paragraph?

_____

_____

3. Choose three phrases in the second paragraph that help to create an image of the tree house.

_____

_____

_____

_____

4. How does the narrator compare the tree house to a person in the fourth paragraph?

_____

_____

5. What does the narrator compare the tree house to in the sixth paragraph?

_____

_____

Point of View

Learn About It

Point of view is the perspective or viewpoint that a **character** or **narrator** has in a story. If the point of view is not directly stated, readers can **infer** it based on how characters act and what they say. Authors often introduce *contrasting* points of view in a text to help establish **conflict** in the **plot**. A character's point of view may also change throughout the course of a story based on the events that take place and the lessons that the character learns.

Look for details in the passage that help to identify Kamisha's point of view. Note how her point of view is connected to her actions.

The alarm clock buzzed at exactly 5 A.M., and Kamisha pulled herself out of bed. The sun was barely rising when she stepped out her front door to begin a long eight-mile run in preparation for the city marathon next month.

It would be a grueling race, and Kamisha knew she had to prepare herself both mentally and physically for it. As her feet hit the pavement, she settled into an easy rhythm and pictured herself crossing the finish line of the race.

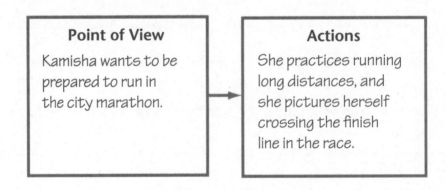

Point of View	Actions
Kamisha wants to be prepared to run in the city marathon.	She practices running long distances, and she pictures herself crossing the finish line in the race.

Try It

Read the passage. Underline the details that help you identify the characters' points of view. Look for details that show how Cole's point of view changes. Use the questions to help you.

Jumping Bean

"**W**ow, will this be a piece of cake," Cole said softly as he surveyed the arena before him. He watched as dogs of different breeds performed their warm-ups over various obstacles around the ring. There were jumps, A-frame ramps, tunnels, and weave poles in this agility competition, and as far as Cole could see, there wasn't one dog that could perform as well as Bean.

> How does Cole feel about the agility competition at the beginning of the story? How do you know?

Looking down proudly at his mixed breed terrier, he laughed when Bean barked at him and winked an eye. It was almost as if he was thinking the same thing.

"We've got this one, buddy," Cole said to his dog, and he gave Bean a reassuring scratch behind his ear. Then they entered the arena to warm up before the competition.

Over the jumps went Bean, clearing every single one of them, and he was *fast*— much faster than any other dog in the ring. Through the tunnel and then off to the weave poles, zigzagging like the pro he was.

Somewhere in the middle of the poles, Cole noticed from the corner of his eye that an excited black-and-white border collie had entered the ring with a female handler. The girl had obviously been watching Bean because she walked right up to Cole and said, "It looks like it's between your dog and mine. Get ready for second place."

> Identify the girl's viewpoint about the competition based on her comments to Cole. How is this point of view different from Cole's?

Continued on the next page ▶

Continued from the previous page

By the time Cole had thought of a response to the rude comment, the girl was already walking away with her dog. He looked down to find that Bean had finished the poles and returned to his side, smiling happily up at him. Not wanting to tire the dog out, Cole walked him outside the ring and gave him a chance to rest and to drink some water.

Cole also wanted to get a look at the border collie to see if he was really as good as the girl had stated. His eyes found the dog midway through the pole sequence, and Cole was surprised to see that he was just as fast as Bean. Then he leaped over a few jumps and made his way up and down the A-frame ramp.

> **Which details indicate that Cole's point of view changes in the story?**

Little beads of sweat began to appear on Cole's forehead, and his hands started to shake. He watched as the border collie sped through the tunnel and shot out the other end like a bullet. Bean suddenly whined loudly.

Looking down, Cole noticed that Bean was watching him and cocking his head to the side. The dog knew something was wrong, but he wasn't sure what it was. Cole didn't want Bean to lose his confidence, so he quickly stopped focusing on the border collie.

"Who's my good boy?!" said Cole excitedly, as he playfully ruffed up Bean's hair. Bean barked in response and happily wagged his tail.

Cole had seen enough to know that it would be a close call between the two dogs. He would just have to try his best and see if Bean would emerge the winner. He and Bean were in for a tough competition, but they were both up for it!

> **Review the end of the story and describe Cole's new point of view toward the competition.**

Explain how plot events in the story affect Cole's point of view. How does his point of view change?

Apply It

Read the passage. Circle details that indicate point of view. Note contrasting points of view and changing points of view in the margin. Answer the questions that follow.

New Year's in Chinatown

It was a cold Sunday morning when Lucas walked down Canal Street in New York City. His friend, Sophie, and her Uncle Robert strolled alongside him, chatting about Chinese New Year.

"Why is everyone wearing red?" asked Sophie, as she looked down the street at the people lining up for the parade. Sophie liked to ask questions . . . a lot of questions.

"Red is a sign of good luck," replied her uncle. "Gold is another color for the New Year. See . . . look at the gold streamers and red-and-gold flags over there." Sophie's uncle pointed to a building down the street, but Lucas kept his eyes down, watching the impressions that his feet made in the thin layer of ice on the ground.

Why Sophie wanted to see the parade in Chinatown was beyond him. They could have gone anywhere else and he would have been happier. This was just another parade, and he didn't even celebrate Chinese New Year.

"And what about those things up there?" Sophie continued. "What are they?"

"Those are paper dragons and red lanterns—they are very common decorations for Chinese New Year," her uncle explained. "You'll see more dragons in the parade, and lions, too." Before Sophie could follow up with another question, her uncle's face suddenly lit up, and he pointed across the street.

Continued on the next page ➤

Continued from the previous page

"Ooh, look over there!" he shouted above the growing noise level of the crowd. "The parade is about to start!"

Lucas glanced up to see a line of colorful floats begin to make their way down the street. All at once, a marching band began to play music and the crowd around him cheered loudly. Dancers seemed to emerge from everywhere in two-, four-, and eight-person costumes. They were dressed as lions and dragons, and they swayed left and right across the street, wishing a year of luck and prosperity to the onlookers. A lion approached Lucas, dancing expertly in front of him; he couldn't help but appreciate the elaborate detail of the costume and the skill of the dancers.

Glancing past the dancers, he saw that acrobats, magicians, and martial artists were making their way toward him. Raising his eyebrows, Lucas realized that this parade was not at all what he expected. The excitement around him was contagious, and he found that he was drawn in by the joyful atmosphere. He stared in wonder at each of the performers, impressed by their particular talents. Looking over at Sophie, he saw that she had a look of fascination on her face, and he wondered if his own face looked like hers.

Later, as the last of the parade passed them by, Sophie's uncle looked down at Lucas and asked, "What did you think?"

Lucas shrugged nonchalantly and answered that it wasn't bad, but he was still cold. Sophie knew better, though, and laughed at his game. Slyly, she asked her uncle, "Don't they have really delicious food during Chinese New Year? Maybe we could pass the food vendors down the block."

Lucas perked up immediately and tried not to look as excited as he felt. Food, after all, was the way to his heart!

Answer these questions about "New Year's in Chinatown." Write your answers in complete sentences.

1. How does Lucas feel at first about going to see the parade in Chinatown?

_____

_____

2. How do Sophie's actions reveal her point of view about Chinese New Year?

_____

_____

3. Contrast Lucas's point of view with Uncle Robert's point of view.

_____

_____

_____

4. Explain how Lucas's point of view changes during the course of the story.

_____

_____

_____

_____

Rhyme, Repetition, and Alliteration

Learn About It

Authors use **literary devices** to affect the meaning, mood, and tone of a text. **Repetition** is an effective device because it draws attention to important words or phrases. Authors also may repeat certain sounds to direct attention. **Rhyme** is the repetition of similar sounds at the ends of lines. Poems usually have a consistent **rhyme scheme**, or rhyming pattern. **Alliteration** is the repetition of beginning consonant sounds.

Read the following stanza from "The Rainy Day" by Henry Wadsworth Longfellow. Look for examples of repetition, rhyme, and alliteration.

> The day is cold, and dark, and dreary;
> It rains, and the wind is never weary;
> The vine still clings to the moldering wall,
> But at every gust the dead leaves fall,
> And the day is dark and dreary.

Repetitive Poetic Devices		
Repetition	**Rhyme**	**Alliteration**
Dark and dreary	Dreary, weary	Day, dark, dreary
	Wall, fall	Wind, weary

Try It

Read the poem. Identify the rhyming words at the ends of lines. Circle them and then label them with A, B, C, and so on. Underline any repetition or alliteration. Use the questions to help you.

adapted from

The Wishing Bridge
by John Greenleaf Whittier

Among the legends sung or said
Along our rocky shore,
The Wishing Bridge of Marblehead
May well be sung once more.

5   A hundred years ago (so ran
The old-time story) all
Good wishes said above its span
Would, soon or late, befall.

If pure and earnest, never failed
10   The prayers of man or maid
For him who on the deep sea sailed,
For her at home who stayed.

Once thereon came two girls from school,
And wished in childish glee
15   And one would be a queen and rule,
And one the world would see.

Time passed; with change of hopes and fears,
And in the self-same place,
Two women, gray with middle years,
20   Stood, wondering, face to face.

With wakened memories, as they met,
They queried what had been
"A poor man's wife am I, and yet,"
Said one, "I am a queen.

> **Look for a rhyme scheme in the poem as you read. Identify it by the letters you label in the margin of the poem. For example, the rhyme scheme in the first stanza is ABAB (*said, shore, head, more*).**

> **The phrase *sung or said* is an example of alliteration in the first line of the poem. Can you find more in the first twenty lines?**

Continued on the next page ➤

Continued from the previous page

25   "My realm a little homestead is,
   Where, lacking crown and throne,
   I rule by loving services
   And patient toil alone."

   The other said: "The great world lies
30   Beyond me as it lay;
   O'er love's and duty's boundaries
   My feet may never stray.

   "I see but common sights of home,
   Its common sounds I hear,
35   My widowed mother's sick-bed room
   Suffices for my sphere.

   "I read to her some pleasant page
   Of travel far and wide,
   And in a dreamy pilgrimage
40   We wander side by side.

   "And when, at last, she falls asleep,
   My book becomes to me
   A magic glass: my watch I keep,
   But all the world I see.

45   "A farm-wife queen your place you fill,
   While fancy's privilege
   Is mine to walk the earth at will,
   Thanks to the Wishing Bridge."

   "Nay, leave the legend for the truth,"
50   The other cried, "and say
   Luck gives the wishes of our youth,
   But in its own best way!"

> Notice how the tenth stanza combines rhyme and alliteration at the end of the lines so that the poem's lines flow into one an other.

> Do any lines or phrases repeat in the poem?

HOTS Evaluate

Which do you think impacts the poem's rhythm more—rhyme or alliteration? Explain why you think so, using examples from the poem.

Apply It

Read the poem. Identify the rhyme scheme using the letters A, B, C, and so on. Circle examples of alliteration and other types of repetition. Answer the questions that follow.

adapted from
39
by Henry Lawson

I only woke this morning
To find the world is fair,
I'm going on for forty,
With scarcely one grey hair;

5   I'm going on for forty,
Where man's strong life begins,
With scarce a sign of crows' feet,
In spite of all my sins.

Then here's the living Forties!
10 The Forties! The Forties!
Then here's the living Forties!
We're good for ten years more.

The teens were black and bitter,
A smothered boyhood's grave,
15 A farm-drudge in the drought-time,
A weary workshop slave.

But twenty years have laid them,
And all the world is fair,
We'll find time in the Forties,
20 To have some boyhood there.

Then here's the wide, free Forties,
The Forties! The Forties!
Then here's the wide, free Forties!
We're good for ten years more!

Continued on the next page ➧

Continued from the previous page

25   The twenties they were noble,
       The bravest years, I feel;
       'Twas man to man in trouble,
       In working and in zeal;

       'Twas man to man in fighting,
30   For money or for praise.
       And we'll find in the Forties
       Some more Bohemian days.

       Then here's the wiser Forties!
       The Forties! The Forties!
35   Then here's the wiser Forties!
       We're good for ten years more.

       The thirties were the fate years;
       I fought behind the scenes.
       The thirties were more cruel
40   And blacker than the teens;

       I held them not but bore them,
       They were no years of mine;
       But they are going from me,
       For I am thirty-nine.

45   So here's the stronger Forties!
       The Forties! The Forties!
       And here's the good old Forties!
       We're good for ten years more.

Answer these questions about "39." Write your answers in complete sentences.

1. What is the rhyme scheme of the first stanza?

_____

_____

2. Give two examples of alliteration in the poem.

_____

_____

_____

_____

3. Explain why certain lines in the poem are repeated. How does this reflect the author's attitude?

_____

_____

_____

_____

4. How does the repetition of sounds impact the rhythm of the poem?

_____

_____

_____

_____

LESSON

9

Poem Structure

Learn About It

There are many kinds of **poetry**. Each style has its own **structure**. A **narrative** poem tells a story. It can be several stanzas long and may follow any rhyme scheme. A **ballad** is written like a song that tells a story. It contains simple stanzas and usually a recurring refrain. A **haiku** is a short, unrhymed, three-line poem with a total of seventeen syllables. The first and third lines have five syllables, and the second line has seven syllables. A **sonnet** has fourteen lines with a fixed rhyme scheme and is usually about love.

Read the following poem. Check the poem against the characteristics in the chart below.

> Winds carry new life
> Seeds in the nurturing earth:
> Green forest rising

Types of Poems	
Poem	**Characteristics**
Haiku	Three unrhymed lines of five, seven, and five syllables each
Sonnet	Fourteen lines with a fixed rhyme scheme
Narrative	Tells a story with characters and a plot
Ballad	Tells a story, written like a song, has simple stanzas and usually a repeating refrain

Try It

Read the poem. Identify its characteristics such as rhyme scheme and line count. Use the questions to help you.

Sonnet 18

by William Shakespeare

Shall I compare thee to a summer's day?
Thou art more lovely and more temperate:
Rough winds do shake the darling buds of May,
And summer's lease hath all too short a date:
5   Sometime too hot the eye of heaven shines,
And often is his gold complexion dimm'd,
And every fair from fair sometime declines,
By chance, or nature's changing course untrimm'd:
But thy eternal summer shall not fade,
10   Nor lose possession of that fair thou ow'st,
Nor shall death brag thou wander'st in his shade,
When in eternal lines to time thou grow'st,
      So long as men can breathe, or eyes can see,
      So long lives this, and this gives life to thee.

> How many lines does the poem have? How does this qualify it as a sonnet?

> What is the topic of this sonnet?

Read the poem. Circle the characteristics that help you identify what kind of poem it is. Use the questions to help you.

excerpted from

The Walrus and the Carpenter
by Lewis Carroll

"O Oysters, come and walk with us!"
The Walrus did beseech.
"A pleasant walk, a pleasant talk,
Along the briny beach:
5   We cannot do with more than four,
To give a hand to each."

The eldest Oyster looked at him,
But never a word he said:
The eldest Oyster winked his eye,
10   And shook his heavy head—
Meaning to say he did not choose
To leave the oyster-bed.

But four young Oysters hurried up,
All eager for the treat:
15   Their coats were brushed, their faces washed,
Their shoes were clean and neat—
And this was odd, because, you know,
They hadn't any feet.
Four other Oysters followed them,
20   And yet another four;
And thick and fast they came at last,
And more, and more, and more—
All hopping through the frothy waves,
     And scrambling to the shore.

> As you read the poem, picture yourself singing it.

How are the two poems structured differently? In what ways do the poems' structures affect their meanings?

54 • Unit 2: Craft and Structure

Apply It

Read the poem. Identify what type of poem it is by its characteristics. Answer the questions that follow.

excerpted and adapted from

The Lady of Shalott
by Alfred, Lord Tennyson

On either side the river lie
Long fields of barley and of rye,
That clothe the world and meet the sky;
And through the field the road runs by
5   To many-towered Camelot;
And up and down the people go,
Gazing where the lilies blow
Round an island there below,
The island of Shalott.

10   Only reapers, reaping early
In among the bearded barley,
Hear a song that echoes cheerly
From the river winding clearly,
Down to towered Camelot:
15   And by the moon the reaper weary,
Piling sheaves in uplands airy,
Listening, whispers "'Tis the fairy
Lady of Shalott."

There she weaves by night and day
20   A magic web with colors gay.
She has heard a whisper say,
A curse is on her if she stay
To look down to Camelot.
She knows not what the curse may be,
25   And so she weaves it steadily,
And little other care hath she,
        The Lady of Shalott.

Continued on the next page ➡

Continued from the previous page

A bow-shot from her bower-eaves,
He rode between the barley-sheaves,
30   The sun came dazzling through the leaves,
And flamed upon the brazen greaves
Of bold Sir Lancelot.
A red-cross knight for ever kneeled
To a lady in his shield,
35   That sparkled on the yellow field,
Beside remote Shalott.

She left the web, she left the loom,
She made three paces through the room,
She saw the water-lily bloom,
40   She saw the helmet and the plume,
She looked down to Camelot.
Out flew the web and floated wide;
The mirror cracked from side to side;
"The curse is come upon me," cried
45   The Lady of Shalott.

Answer these questions about "The Lady of Shalott." Write your answers in complete sentences.

1. How is the poem similar to a story?

_____

_____

_____

_____

2. What do the first two stanzas of the poem describe?

_____

3. Who are the characters in the poem?

_____

_____

4. What is the rhyming pattern in the poem?

_____

_____

5. What kind of poem is "The Lady of Shalott"? How do you know?

_____

_____

_____

_____

Drama Structure

Learn About It

> A **drama** is meant to be performed by actors for an audience. A drama has many parts. The **cast of characters** is a list of who is in the play. **Dialogue** is the conversation between characters. A **monologue** is when one character speaks at length to another. A **soliloquy** is when a character is alone on stage and thinks aloud. An **act** is made up of scenes. A **scene** has a fixed setting and continuous time frame. **Stage directions** tell actors what to do. Stage directions are in *italic* print.

Read the stage directions and the soliloquy. Use the chart to help you understand the purpose of each.

Setting: Lihua enters her bedroom from the rear of the stage, wearing a nightgown and robe. The full moon shines through her window; there are no stars in the sky. Lihua walks slowly toward the window-seat at her window and sits down, facing the audience. She is deep in thought.

LIHUA: (*looking up at the moon*) Tomorrow will determine my fate. Will I marry Chenglei, or will I fulfill my destiny and become the leader that my people need? How can I contradict the wishes of my parents, who have protected and guided me? But how can I act against my heart, knowing what is truly right? Tomorrow, my life will change. I only hope I have the courage to choose the more difficult path.

Element	Meaning	Example
Character	Who is in the drama	Lihua
Stage directions	What the character does	Lihua enters her bedroom from the rear of the stage, wearing a nightgown and robe. (looking up at the moon)
Soliloquy	A character alone onstage speaks to herself	Tomorrow will determine my fate. Will I marry Chenglei, or will I fulfill my destiny and become the leader that my people need?

Try It

Read the passage. Identify dramatic elements and write the name of the element in the margin, next to the text. Use the questions to help you.

excerpted and adapted from

The Importance of Being Earnest
by Oscar Wilde

Use the stage direction at the beginning of the passage to help you visualize the setting.

ACT I

Algernon Moncrieff's Flat in Half-Moon Street, W.

Setting: Morning-room in Algernon's flat in Half-Moon Street. The room is luxuriously and artistically furnished. The sound of a piano is heard from the adjoining room.

Lane is arranging afternoon tea on the table, and after the music has ceased, Algernon enters.

ALGERNON: Did you hear what I was playing, Lane?

LANE: I didn't think it polite to listen, sir.

ALGERNON: I'm sorry for that, for your sake. I don't play accurately—anyone can play accurately—but I play with wonderful expression. As far as the piano is concerned, sentiment is my forte. I keep science for Life.

LANE: Yes, sir.

Identify the narration as dialogue, monologue, or a soliloquy. How do you know which it is?

ALGERNON: And, speaking of the science of Life, have you got the cucumber sandwiches cut for Lady Bracknell?

LANE: Yes, sir. (*produces the sandwiches on a tray*)

Algernon inspects them, takes two, and sits down on the sofa. Lane goes out. Lane re-enters.

LANE: Mr. Ernest Worthing.

Enter Jack. Lane goes out.

ALGERNON: How are you, my dear Ernest? What brings you up to town?

JACK: Oh, pleasure, pleasure! What else should bring one anywhere? Eating as usual, I see, Algy!

ALGERNON: (*stiffly*) I believe it is customary in good society to take some slight refreshment at five o'clock. Where have you been since last Thursday?

JACK: (*sitting down on the sofa*) In the country.

Continued on the next page ➤

Continued from the previous page

ALGERNON: What on earth do you do there?

JACK: (*pulling off his gloves*) When one is in town, one amuses oneself. When one is in the country, one amuses other people. It is excessively boring.

ALGERNON: And who are the people you amuse?

JACK: (*airily*) Oh, neighbors, neighbors.

ALGERNON: Got nice neighbors in your part of Shropshire?

JACK: Perfectly horrid! Never speak to one of them.

ALGERNON: How immensely you must amuse them! (*goes over and takes sandwich*) By the way, Shropshire is your county, is it not?

JACK: Eh? Shropshire? Yes, of course. Hallo! Why all these cups? Why cucumber sandwiches? Why such reckless extravagance in one so young? Who is coming to tea?

ALGERNON: Oh, merely Aunt Augusta and Gwendolen.

JACK: How perfectly delightful!

ALGERNON: Yes, that is all very well; but I am afraid Aunt Augusta won't quite approve of your being here.

JACK: May I ask why?

ALGERNON: My dear fellow, the way you flirt with Gwendolen is perfectly disgraceful. It is almost as bad as the way Gwendolen flirts with you.

JACK: I am in love with Gwendolen. I have come up to town expressly to propose to her.

ALGERNON: I thought you had come up for pleasure. I call that business.

JACK: How utterly unromantic you are!

ALGERNON: I really don't see anything romantic in proposing. It is very romantic to be in love. But there is nothing romantic about a definite proposal. Why, one may be accepted. One usually is, I believe. Then the excitement is all over. The very essence of romance is uncertainty. If ever I get married, I'll certainly try to forget the fact.

JACK: I have no doubt about that, dear Algy. The Divorce Court was specially invented for people whose memories are so curiously constituted.

> **What have you learned about the characters based on their conversation?**

> **After you finish reading, go back to review the different elements and how they relate to each other.**

HOTS Apply

Suppose the author added a monologue to the end of this excerpt. What would Jack likely say to Algernon?

Apply It

Read the passage. Ask yourself questions about the elements of drama and how they function in this play. Answer the questions that follow.

excerpted and adapted from

Getting Married

by George Bernard Shaw

Setting: The kitchen is occupied at present by Mrs. Bridgenorth, who is talking to Mr. William Collins, the greengrocer. He is in evening dress, though it is early forenoon. Mrs. Bridgenorth is a quiet, happy-looking woman of fifty. Collins is an elderly man. He is at the oak chest counting a pile of napkins.

Mrs. Bridgenorth reads placidly; Collins counts; a blackbird sings in the garden. Mrs. Bridgenorth puts The Times *down in her lap and considers Collins for a moment.*

MRS. BRIDGENORTH: Do you never feel nervous on these occasions, Collins?

COLLINS: Lord bless you, no, ma'am. It would be a joke, after marrying five of your daughters, if I was to get nervous over marrying the last of them.

MRS. BRIDGENORTH: I have always said you were a wonderful man, Collins.

COLLINS: (*almost blushing*) Oh, ma'am!

MRS. BRIDGENORTH: Yes. I never could arrange anything—a wedding or even dinner—without some hitch or other.

COLLINS: Why should you give yourself the trouble, ma'am? Send for the greengrocer, ma'am: that's the secret of easy housekeeping.

MRS. BRIDGENORTH: What a bond between us, Collins! You will superintend the breakfast yourself as usual, of course, won't you?

COLLINS: Yes, yes, bless you, ma'am, of course. I always do. Them fashionable caterers send down such people as I never did set eyes on. Dukes you would take them for. You see the relatives shaking hands with them and asking them about the family—actually ladies saying "Where have we met before?" and all sorts of confusion. That's my secret in business, ma'am. You can always spot me as the greengrocer. It's a fortune to me in these days, when you can't hardly tell who anyone is or isn't. (*he goes out through the tower, and immediately returns for a moment to announce*) The General, ma'am.

Continued on the next page ➤

Continued from the previous page

Mrs. Bridgenorth rises to receive her brother-in-law, who enters in full-dress uniform, with many medals and decorations. He comes to the hearth, where Mrs. Bridgenorth is standing with her back to the fireplace.

MRS. BRIDGENORTH: *Good morning, Boxer. (They shake hands.) Another niece to give away. This is the last of them.*

THE GENERAL: (*very gloomy*) Yes, Alice. Nothing for the old warrior uncle to do but give away brides to luckier men than himself. Has—(*he chokes*) has your sister come yet?

MRS. BRIDGENORTH: (*going to him*) Oh come, Boxer! Really, really! We are no longer boys and girls. You can't keep up a broken heart all your life. It must be nearly twenty years since she refused you. And you know that it's not because she dislikes you, but only that she's not a marrying woman.

THE GENERAL: It's no use. I love her still. And I can't help telling her so whenever we meet, though I know it makes her avoid me. (*He all but weeps.*)

MRS. BRIDGENORTH: What does she say when you tell her?

THE GENERAL: Only that she wonders when I am going to grow out of it. I know now that I shall never grow out of it.

MRS. BRIDGENORTH: Perhaps you would if you married her. I believe you're better as you are, Boxer.

Curtain falls.

Answer these questions about "Getting Married." Write your answers in complete sentences.

1. How do the descriptions of the characters in the beginning of the drama help you form an opinion about them?

_____

_____

2. This excerpt has only one act and one scene. Based on this, what do you expect about the setting of the remainder of the play?

_____

_____

3. What do you learn about Collins from his monologue?

_____

_____

4. What does this excerpt reveal about the General?

_____

_____

5. How would your impression of the scene be different if there were no stage directions?

_____

_____

_____

_____

Fictional Portrayals of Characters

Learn About It

Fictional texts may be based on real people. For example, a story may be written about a famous person in history. However, all of the events and descriptions in the story are not likely true. It is helpful to compare and contrast an **autobiography** or **biography** about a person's life with the fictional story about the person. In this way, readers can identify similarities and differences between nonfiction and fiction. It also helps readers understand how authors use or alter facts when writing fiction.

Read the story about Jackie Robinson. Review the Venn diagram to see which parts of the story really happened and which parts are fiction.

The crowd cheered as Jackie Robinson's bat made contact with the ball and a loud CRACK echoed through the stadium. Every single person rose from their seats to cheer for the great baseball player. He had only played in the major leagues for a few months, but he was already a hero.

As Kyle watched his idol round the bases, he thought that it was no wonder everyone loved Jackie. His story was an inspirational one that related to us all in some way.

Jackie Robinson's Life

Early in Jackie's baseball career, many people did not want him to play in the major leagues.

Both

Jackie was a great baseball player who had many fans.

Story about Jackie Robinson

Everyone in the stadium loved Jackie.

Try It

Read the two passages about Leif Eriksson, a famous Viking. Underline the similarities between the passages and circle the differences. Use the questions to help you.

Leif Eriksson

Leif Eriksson was a Viking explorer born in Iceland around the year 975. His father was Erik the Red, an explorer who started the first European settlement of Greenland. As a boy, Leif went to live with his father in Greenland until the year 1000. Then he returned to the land of his ancestors in Norway. Many believe that he was converted to Christianity while in Norway, and King Olaf sent him back to Greenland to convert the natives there. Leif left Norway with the intention of returning to Greenland, but what happened next is a subject of debate.

Some stories say that Leif's sailing vessel was blown off course and, as a result, he became the first European to land in North America (in Newfoundland, Canada). Other stories say that another Viking, Bjarni Herjulfsson, had already been to North America, and Leif purchased his vessel with the intention of purposely following the same route. If this second story is true, Leif was *not* the first European to land in North America.

Leif eventually did return to Greenland, and no doubt told his tale to the people there. He died around 1020 at about the age of 45.

It is a mystery whether Leif Eriksson reached North America intentionally, by mistake, or even at all. He may or may not have been the first European to touch the ground in this new land. But regardless of the lack of proof, he is widely regarded as one of the most famous Vikings in history.

> As you read, look for important facts about Leif Eriksson: When and where did he live? What was he famous for?

> Note that there are different ideas about Leif Eriksson's journey to North America. Compare this with the story you will read next.

An Unexpected Landing

The long, sleek ship cut through the waves as the Viking shouted to his men to row the ship into the wind. Relentlessly, the angry storm blew, thwarting the efforts of the strong sailors who tried to steer the ship. Leif Eriksson looked on helplessly as the wind slowly gained ground in this elemental tug-of-war, and the ship started to turn.

What does the beginning of the story describe? How is this different from the biography?

In response, Leif shouted at the men to regroup and double their efforts, cursing nature for its cruel intent; but the shrill winds simply carried his voice out to the farthest reaches of the sea as yet another wave crashed into the vessel. Defeated, Leif was forced to let the wind push and pull where it would. His journey back to Greenland would hopefully end soon, for King Olaf was counting on him.

Days later, Leif discovered that nature was not as cruel as it was kind, for before him lay a world unknown, previously untouched by him or anyone else he knew of. It was a new world, but one similar to his own. It had ice and watery shores, but it also had wide expanses of land—land that could be settled, just as his father had settled Greenland. His friend, Ulf, helped him explore this new land, and together they saw the future in every step they took.

"Ulf, did you know that such a world could exist?" Leif would repeat in wonder. "And so far from our homes and families?"

Ulf merely nodded, speechless as he sifted the soil between his large fingers. He scooped some up with his hand and placed it in a pouch so that others would believe their story.

Look for connections as you read the story, such as the mention of King Olaf in both passages.

Continued on the next page ➡

With high hopes, Leif and his men began the long journey back to Greenland. Leif had originally intended to preach Christianity to the Greenland natives, but now he also had a secondary motive for returning. For long days and nights, the men rowed, eager to return to familiar land. Finally they arrived to find the small settlement where Leif's father lived.

> Which parts of the story are supported by the facts in the biography?

Anxiously, Leif sought out his father, Erik the Red, longing to announce his discovery. But when he told his father, he was rewarded with a guarded look and lack of interest. Desperate, Leif attempted to explain the possibilities in this new world.

"You of all people should understand the value of settlements," explained Leif, his voice rising in excitement. "Why won't you travel with me to see this place for yourself?"

But his father replied that his home was here in Greenland, and that was where he belonged. Even when Ulf approached them and showed the soil in his pouch, Erik the Red would not be swayed.

News of Leif's discovery traveled through the settlement, but Leif saw fear of the unknown replace what used to be a longing for adventure. He vowed that he would one day return to the new land, even if he had to do it alone. Perhaps when he returned to Norway, King Olaf would help him organize a vessel and crew. For now, he was resigned to do his duty for the king and bide his time. He knew, though, that his day would come.

> Notice that Leif's intentions to settle the new land are discussed in the story, but not in the biography. Why would the author include those fictional details?

HOTS Understand

Compare the ways that Leif Eriksson is portrayed in the two passages. In which passage do you get a better idea of what Eriksson was like as a person? Why?

Apply It

Read the two passages about Calamity Jane, a frontier woman known for her sharpshooting and excellent horseback riding skills. Look for similarities and differences between the passages. Answer the questions that follow.

Calamity Jane (1852–1903)

Calamity Jane was born in 1852, in Missouri. When she was thirteen years old, her family traveled by stagecoach to Montana. During the five-month journey, Jane became an exceptional rider and learned to hunt with the men.

Jane traveled a lot in her early life. After her mother died in Montana, the family moved to Utah, where her father died unexpectedly. At just fourteen years old, Jane was left to care for her five younger siblings. She moved them to Wyoming, where she worked odd jobs to support the family.

Jane earned her nickname "Calamity Jane" when she and some troops were ambushed by a group of Native Americans. According to Jane, the captain was the first to be shot. As Jane was galloping away, she turned to see him fall from his horse. Heedless of the danger, she turned her horse and rode into the attack, where she lifted the captain onto her horse and escaped.

Jane was also a brave rider on the Pony Express, delivering mail across fifty miles of wild country. Later, she was a rider and sharpshooter in Buffalo Bill's Wild West Show.

Jane was tough, but she was also known to have a soft heart. She was prospecting for gold in Deadwood, Wyoming, when a smallpox plague struck the mining town. Jane singlehandedly nursed many of the residents, including children, back to health.

Calamity Jane died in 1903. She was a rough cowgirl with a kind heart, and she lived for the adventure that could only be found in the Old West.

A Witness to Greatness

James rode next to Jane as the group of horsemen traveled back to camp. They had been sent out to control an uprising of Native Americans near Goose Creek, Wyoming. Captain Egan had led the troops on a successful mission, but they had lost six of their soldiers, and the troops were weary as they headed back to camp.

James turned to see that Jane had closed her eyes and was resting quietly on her horse. Although she could obviously never be a soldier like himself, he had been impressed with her riding skills, and she was an excellent shot with a rifle. More than once, he had watched as she hit her target from a distance farther than he would normally expect . . . especially for a woman. He and the rest of the troops were still trying to figure her out. She was a woman, but she dressed and acted like a cowboy— and a darn good one at that.

James had just noted the distance to camp—about a mile and a half to go—when he heard the unmistakable sound of an ambush from the left flank of the troops. Looking up, James saw a group of Native Americans on horseback racing toward them. Their gunfire split the silence of the Wyoming plains. The group was large . . . much larger than anything that the troops could handle in their condition. James knew that reinforcements would be sent once the camp saw the charge from a distance.

James turned to Jane to tell her to run, but she was already at the head of the group, racing with the wind at her back. Shaking his head in awe, he maneuvered over to Captain Egan to protect his left side. Before he could get in position though, the sound of gunfire—much closer now—whizzed by. James watched as Captain Egan fell from his horse, obviously struck by a bullet. Confusion reigned, and horses and riders were everywhere; they all seemed to be in the direct path to the captain, and James watched helplessly as Egan lay motionless on the ground not twenty feet away.

Just when he thought all hope was lost, James watched as Jane's

Continued on the next page ➤

Continued from the previous page

horse galloped toward the captain, head down and ears pinned as Jane crouched low over his neck. Her hat had fallen back and her hair flew wildly in the wind. At first, James thought that she was planning to take on the Native Americans by herself, but he quickly realized that she aimed to rescue the captain.

In a heroic moment, James witnessed Jane rein her horse up to the captain and lift him onto the saddle in front of her. Ducking gunfire, she pushed her horse to run as fast as his feet could carry him, and amazingly, she escaped unharmed.

James wouldn't have believed it if he hadn't seen it with his own eyes. Urging his horse forward, he chased the quickly diminishing horse with two riders in front of him. He only hoped he made it back to camp alive so that he could tell the amazing tale of Calamity Jane!

Answer these questions about "Calamity Jane (1852–1903)" and "A Witness to Greatness." Write your answers in complete sentences.

1. Which information in "A Witness to Greatness" is supported by facts in "Calamity Jane (1852–1903)"?

_____

_____

2. Which information in the story is not supported by facts in the biography?

_____

_____

3. Both passages tell how Calamity Jane got her nickname. How does the tale differ from the information in the biography?

_____

_____

_____

_____

4. How does the author of "A Witness to Greatness" want you to view Calamity Jane? How do you know?

_____

_____

_____

_____

Fictional Portrayals of Time

Learn About It

Fictional texts may center around a specific time period in history, such as the Industrial Revolution. Some details and events are true to the time period, but some are not. **Comparing and contrasting** historical fiction with actual facts about the time period helps readers understand how and why authors manipulate facts when writing fiction.

Read the story about the California Gold Rush in the mid-19th century. Review the Venn diagram to see which parts of the story accurately reflect the time period and which do not.

Annie diligently watched the pan as she shook it, her eyes searching for the telltale signs of gold. Sighing, she dropped the pan at the side of the river and paused to take a drink of water. All around her, people were anxiously looking at their own pans. A million people had flocked to California once news of Marshall's gold nugget had spread across the country. How could she ever expect to get rich when there was so much competition around her?

The California Gold Rush
Three hundred thousand people came searching for gold.

Both
People panned for gold at rivers in California.

Story about the California Gold Rush
One million people came searching for gold.

Try It

Read the two passages about the Great Depression. Underline the similarities between the passages and circle the differences. Use the questions to help you.

The Great Depression

The Great Depression was an economic crisis that affected market economies across the world. In the United States, it began with the stock market crash in 1929, and lasted through the 1930s. The United States economy, in particular, suffered during the Great Depression, and many people lost their jobs. In 1933, twenty-five percent of all workers were out of work. Farm workers fared better than others. About thirty-seven percent of all non-farm workers were unemployed.

What is the greatest impact that the Great Depression had on the people of the United States?

Many people struggled to stay alive during this time period. Families lost their homes because they could no longer pay their mortgages. People moved across the country in the false hope that work could be found in places like California or New York. Simple necessities such as bread, eggs, and milk were considered luxuries, and sadly, some people starved.

How was the Great Depression a global crisis?

Because of the significant impact of the Great Depression and the very slow recovery of the economy, the federal government took some measures to intervene. Two main results of this changing role in government were the creation of Social Security and unemployment benefits. These programs provided money for the elderly who could not work and for those who were involuntarily unemployed.

The Great Depression impacted not only the United States, but other countries such as Poland, Brazil, Germany, Argentina, and Canada, as well as Southeast Asia. The onset of World War II finally improved the United States economy, but the Great Depression will always be remembered as one of the worst periods in U.S. history.

Emily's Secret

Emily tiptoed down the dim stairway and knocked on Matilda's bedroom door. The sleepy woman opened it a crack and yawned silently.

"Is it morning already?" Matilda asked, but she already knew the answer. Shutting the door, she pulled on one of two dresses she owned and shrugged into her only coat. When she opened the door again, Emily was still there, waiting.

"Please hurry, Matilda," Emily pleaded in a whisper. "I don't want to be late."

"Okay, sweetie," Matilda replied quietly. "I'm coming."

As the pair stepped into the predawn darkness and walked down the sidewalk, Emily told Matilda about the latest dream she had last night.

"Papa had gotten his job back at the bank, and Mama didn't have to sew clothes for a living anymore . . . and I dreamed that you were able to find a job, Matilda . . . wouldn't that be nice?"

Matilda nodded silently and stared at the sidewalk in front of her. She had lost her job as a secretary when the stock market crashed last year, and now that the depression had hit, she could find nothing. It was only by the kind hearts of Emily's parents that Matilda was not homeless. They had taken her in, even though she had been a total stranger to them.

Matilda looked down at the top of Emily's head and draped her arm around her shoulder. Emily was as good-hearted as her parents. She had been afraid at first to ask Matilda for the favor of walking her to the town market every morning, but it was the least that Matilda could do for the family. Emily's only other request was to keep their daily morning walk a secret from her parents.

> What does the description of Matilda's clothing suggest? How does this relate to actual facts about the Great Depression?

> What do you learn about the characters from Emily's description of her dream?

Continued on the next page ▶

Later that evening, Emily's father returned home from another day of job-hunting. His face was drawn and tired, and his shoulders were stooped in defeat. Emily's mother tried to hide her response, but Emily could see the pain in her eyes. She stood by the kitchen door, half-hidden, while her mother spoke in low tones to her father.

> Compare what you learned in the first passage to the details in the story. Which text did you underline?

"The bank called again today, Robert. They're coming for the money tomorrow, and they said . . . they said that if we don't have it, they will take the house."

Emily's eyes widened, and her heart raced at the thought of losing her home.

"How much more do we need?" replied her father in a weary tone.

"Fifty dollars," she answered. "Can you believe that we will lose our home for fifty dollars?"

"Wait!" Emily blurted. She ran into the kitchen as her mother quickly turned away to dab her eyes. "Please, wait! I have the money."

> It would have been unlikely for Emily to have a job during this time period. Why do you think the author included it in the story?

"What?" her father asked in disbelief. "How?"

"I've been working at Millman's Market in the morning before school. Matilda has been walking me there every day. I wanted to save some money for when we really needed it. Is this a good time to use it?"

Emily's father laughed in relief as her mother quickly hugged her. "Yes, my darling," she choked. "It's the perfect time to use it, and you are the perfect daughter for thinking of it."

How did the Great Depression affect family life on a daily basis?

Apply It

Read the two passages about the Middle Ages, a time period from the 5th to the 15th century. Look for similarities and differences between the passages. Answer the questions that follow.

The Medieval Class System

The Middle Ages, or Medieval times, had a well-defined class system. A king, or lord, ruled large sections of land. He divided his land into *fiefs*, and gave it to *vassals*, or local lords, to help protect and manage the property. The vassals had *serfs*, or peasants who lived in a lord's manor. Serfs were bound to the manor and could not leave it or even marry without the lord's permission. Serfs worked on the manor, but they also had small plots of land that were their own. Vassals also had *servants*, or peasants who worked inside the lord's manor house.

Knights were warriors and noblemen who pledged themselves as vassals to the king. They were often given their own land. Boys as young as seven years old became *pages*, and learned social skills. They became *squires* when they were thirteen or fourteen years old, at which point they assisted knights and practiced fighting on horseback. Once they were twenty-one years old, they usually became knights.

Noblewomen were the wives and daughters of noblemen. They raised children and supervised the servants of the household. Their days usually consisted of household activities, and they rarely left the home. Noblewomen were in charge of the manor while their husbands were away.

If you were not a peasant, nobleman, or noblewoman, you were likely a *merchant* who sold goods in medieval towns, or possibly a wandering *minstrel* who sang songs for money. You might also be a member of the church, which was the center of life during the Middle Ages.

How Wonderful It Must Be

"Hello, Sir Edgar."

"Hello, Lady Alison."

Alison giggled happily as she appeared from the wooded forest that surrounded her father's manor. She stepped into the sunshine and raised her head to the clouds. Edgar laughed beside her. He was a few years younger than Alison and had not yet become a squire, but she found she could always count on him to keep her company whenever she had time to take these walks.

Dancing in circles, she stopped every so often to pluck some wildflowers along the edge of the forest. Gallantly, she offered them to Edgar, and he blushed a deep red.

"Oh, how I wish I could be a knight like you will be, Edgar," said Alison.

"But why? You're a girl," Edgar replied.

Alison sighed and gave him a small smile, but she did not answer. Instead, she absently wrapped her blonde braid around her wrist and smoothed the ruffles in her dress. Edgar didn't know that she was thinking of adventure—of knights on horseback and daring swordfights, of battles for the king and journeys to faraway and exotic places. No, Edgar thought that Alison was thinking of her needlework and tea, and lessons in the kitchen.

Continued on the next page ➡

Continued from the previous page

He wandered closer to a babbling brook and tossed a few pebbles in the stream. Soon, he became lost in his own thoughts. Would he be a good squire for Sir Alfred? Would he embarrass himself on the training field and fall off his horse? Glancing at Alison, he realized that she was a much more accomplished rider than he was. How could he ever become a knight? For a moment, he let his mind wander to the merchants he had seen in town while on errands last week. How wonderful it must be to be a free man without the pressures of nobility constantly crushing you! He imagined that he would enjoy selling wares in town . . . much more than fighting battles on horseback.

"Why don't we walk a little farther down the way?" Alison suggested, but she already knew what Edgar's response would be.

"We can't! There could be highwaymen waiting to capture us and hold us for ransom!" Alison laughed at Edgar. "Where's your sense of adventure, *Sir* Edgar?" she teased.

Sulking, Edgar led the way down the dirt path as Alison enjoyed the late afternoon sun shining through the overhead leaves. From a distance, she could see the peasants working hard as they plowed their plots of land. She thought of Myrna, the peasant-girl who had become her good friend. Myrna had been busy helping her family the past few weeks, so Alison had not seen much of her. She wondered if she was down there now, working hard under the setting sun.

Finally, as the sun began to disappear, the two friends turned for home. Before they parted ways, Alison made Edgar promise to meet her again. Then, as she looked up at the imposing manor house before her, she sighed in resignation and entered the main hall.

Answer these questions about "The Medieval Class System" and "How Wonderful It Must Be." Write your answers in complete sentences.

1. How does Alison in "How Wonderful It Must Be" differ from the typical noblewoman described in "The Medieval Class System"?

_____

_____

2. How old is Edgar in the story, based on the information in both passages? Explain how you know.

_____

_____

3. Why is it unusual that Edgar would prefer to be a merchant rather than a knight?

_____

4. Is it odd that Alison is a more accomplished rider than Edgar? Use the first passage to help you explain your answer.

_____

_____

5. Why do you think the author of the story included information about Myrna, even though noblewomen were probably not friends with peasants during the Middle Ages?

_____

_____

_____

_____

Fictional Portrayals of Places

Learn About It

Fictional texts may be based on real places, such as the Eiffel Tower or the Sahara Desert. Details about the place may include a mixture of fact and fiction. It is helpful to **compare and contrast** reliable information about the place with the fictional story about it. This can help readers understand how authors alter facts when writing fiction.

Read the story about the legend of the Fountain of Youth. Review the Venn diagram to see which parts of the story are fact and which parts are fiction.

For hours, the conquistadors had searched the vegetation of the island of Bimini, when one of Ponce de Leon's men sent word that he had found the spring—the fountain that would restore youth to any who drinks from it.

Excitedly, Ponce de Leon listened to the directions and set out on foot for this magical place, but in a twist of fate, he was shot by an arrow from an island native.

Quickly, his men returned him to his ship and they set sail for Cuba. He would later die of his wounds, never to see the legendary Fountain of Youth that he had yearned to find.

The Fountain of Youth
Ponce de Leon never discovered it.

Both
Ponce de Leon sought to find the Fountain of Youth on Bimini.

Story about the Fountain of Youth
Ponce de Leon learned of its location.

Try It

Read the two passages about the Eiffel Tower in Paris. Underline the similarities between the passages and circle the differences. Use the questions to help you.

The Eiffel Tower

The Eiffel Tower is one of the most visited landmarks in the world. Hundreds of millions of people have come to Paris, France, to see this iron monument. The tower, however, was not quite so popular when it was being constructed.

Alexandre Gustave Eiffel designed the tower in 1884 in the hopes of unveiling it at the International Exhibition of France. The exhibition would take place in 1889, commemorating the 100-year anniversary of the French Revolution. Eiffel's tower was chosen out of 700 proposed designs, and construction began in 1887.

Almost immediately, people were against the project. Their arguments varied. Some said that the task was too daunting and the tower would never be completed in time. Others thought that the cost of the structure was much too high. Some even believed that it would be an eyesore in their beautiful city.

Despite the critics' complaints, Eiffel was able to complete construction of the tower in time for the exhibition. Within a mere twenty-one months, he individually crafted 12,000 iron pieces and carefully fitted them together like a jigsaw puzzle. Eiffel was a talented engineer and had previous experience working with other metal structures. He and his workers shaped every piece perfectly before bolting them together. The resulting tower stood 1,000 feet high.

In the end, Eiffel's tower was a huge success. Even his harshest critics could not ignore that the project had run smoothly, quickly, and safely. Today, the Eiffel Tower is the defining landmark of Paris. It is hard to picture the city without this incredible structure.

> Look at the details in the second and third paragraphs. Remember to check these details against the story on the next page.

> In what ways is the Eiffel Tower unique and impressive?

Building a Work of Art

It seemed only yesterday that I had begun work on Eiffel's tower, yet here I am almost two years later at its completion. I stand in line with the other iron workers, dressed in my finest as the city introduces this man-made wonder. I cannot help but tip my hat to the genius behind it all.

Gustave Eiffel steps forward to shake the hands of numerous city officials. There are other engineers nearby, but I had the honor of working with Eiffel directly. If only every employer were as easy to work with! Metalworking is a difficult and sometimes frustrating trade, but Eiffel had patience like I'd never seen before. Twelve thousand iron pieces! Every piece was carefully handcrafted to fit, and then bolted together. It was no wonder that he had so many workers on his team, yet everyone worked together like a well-oiled machine. I can't remember the last time a project had gone so smoothly.

Sneaking a glance, I tilt my head back to see the amazing structure touch the sky. It stands thousands of feet above me, seemingly rising forever. How did we possibly accomplish this in twenty-one months? I laugh despite myself, and Frederic elbows me in the ribs. I scowl at my fellow worker, but continue to feel amazement and pride at this feat.

In the second paragraph, the narrator says that Eiffel was easy to work with and had great patience. Why might the author want to exaggerate these traits in the story?

What other fact about the Eiffel Tower is exaggerated in the third paragraph? Why?

Continued on the next page

Turning, I see the crowd of Parisians, their heads also tilted backward as they stare in wonder. I watch newspaper reporters—the same ones who viciously attacked Eiffel's tower not more than a few months prior—standing eagerly now, waiting for a chance to congratulate him. I also see overstuffed businessmen with their shiny shoes, nodding their heads in agreement, as if they knew all along that the tower would be a success. Weren't these the very same men who sent letters to the papers and signed petitions to halt the project? Didn't they say that it would be a disaster, a blemish on our fair city?

Frowning, I suddenly notice that those same reporters and businessmen are looking at me and applauding. Frederic is smiling with his toothless grin and patting me on the back. Belatedly, I realize that Eiffel has mentioned me in his speech, and has given me credit in particular for my work. I feel my face grow hot and my hands begin to sweat. I cannot remember ever being recognized for my work, let alone so publicly.

> Think about why the author might want to include Eiffel's public acknowledgment of the narrator, even if it were not supported by facts.

As the celebration ends and the crowd begins to thin, I feel the need to approach Eiffel one last time. I shake his hand and, as we say good-bye, I sense that he feels just as I do—that only we few can truly claim this structure as our own, for we stood by it from the very beginning and never doubted our ability to succeed while all around us thought we'd fail. Walking away, I feel both pride in my achievement and sadness that it is over. I know that I will never build another structure that will mean half as much as this one.

> The narrator says that "all around us thought we'd fail" in the last paragraph. How does this description differ from the first passage?

HOTS Evaluate

Which passage gives the reader a better sense of what it is like to view the Eiffel Tower? How does the author create that effect?

Apply It

Read the two passages about Easter Island, an island in the Pacific Ocean off the coast of South America. Look for similarities and differences between the passages. Answer the questions that follow.

The Mystery of Easter Island

Easter Island is located 2,200 miles west of Chile in South America. It is about 14 miles long by 7 miles wide. The island is best known for more than 600 huge stone statues that vary in height from 10 to 40 feet and can weigh as much as 80 tons. Archaeologists have estimated that the statues were erected between the years 1000 and 1600, but little else is known about them.

Europeans first arrived at Easter Island in 1722, where they saw people of mixed ethnicities who appeared to be worshiping these statues. In 1770, a Spanish expedition estimated that about 3,000 people were on the island. A civil war seems to have occurred within the next four years, because when the British arrived in 1774, there was a much smaller population, and most of the statues had been purposely toppled over.

Many archaeologists believe that the statues represent important people who were immortalized after they died. Archaeologists think that the natives carved most of each statue at a volcano on the island, and then transported it using wooden logs. The statues were likely tipped over as a result of a civil war between two distinct cultures on the island. The culture that worshiped the statues was apparently defeated, and the victorious culture destroyed the statues.

No one knows exactly what happened at Easter Island, but there is no doubt that the statues seem to tell a haunting tale. The island's mysterious beauty draws visitors to see the statues for themselves . . . and to come to their own conclusions.

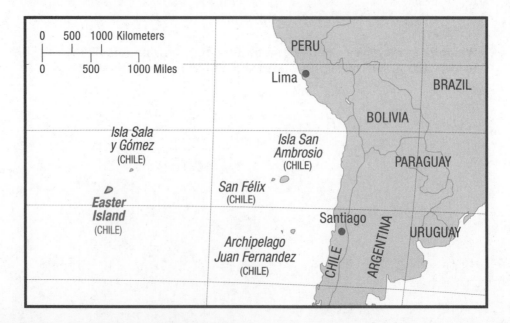

The Island of the Statues

The plane landed neatly on the airstrip, and Celine patiently waited for it to come to a stop. Her little brother, Russ, leaned over her to press his nose against the glass window. He reminded her of a little puppy, and she was immediately annoyed.

"Russ, you're crushing me!" she complained.

"Oh, please," he replied. "You got to look out the window the whole trip."

Celine didn't see this as a bonus, considering she wasn't very fond of heights.

"All right, kids," announced their father. "It looks like we're about to exit the plane, and I need to find my contact . . . I think his name is . . . "

Celine's father fished around in his soft briefcase. He had a tendency to lose track of things, but as far as archaeology was concerned, he was considered to be one of the best. He had a short job here at Easter Island, and he had asked the kids to come along since it was the middle of their summer vacation.

"You're sitting on the handle of my bag," barked Celine at her brother.

"Well, who told you to put it on my seat?" answered Russ, smirking at his own brilliance.

"PIERRE!" announced their father, smiling at the two kids. It took Celine a moment to realize that her father was talking about his contact from the museum.

A few hours later, the family had found Pierre and was being driven to the archaeological site. Celine and Russ were told that they could help out with some light work, and run errands for the team.

As the car rolled toward the site, Celine and Russ were (for once) not bickering. Perhaps it was because the scenery had made them speechless. Everywhere they looked, they were confronted with huge stone statues—face after face of incredible artistry and skill.

"Dad?" Russ asked, a little uncertainly.

"Hmm?"

"What on earth are these things?!" Celine blurted.

"Oh! I didn't tell you about the stone statues?" he replied. "These are about a thousand years old, and they're likely religious idols that were worshiped by the natives.

Continued on the next page ➤

There is a lot of mystery surrounding them. For instance, it's a mystery as to exactly how they were transported and erected around the island."

Celine loved mysteries, and her mind was already working. "Well, they probably used a technique similar to the Ancient Egyptians—maybe wood logs or planks . . . "

Russ rolled his eyes.

"How heavy are the statues?" she continued, unaware that her brother was making fun of her.

"Well, the heaviest ones are around 80 tons," her father replied.

Celine sat silently in her seat and tried to calculate the possibilities. She needed to get a bit more information about these statues, such as how tall they were and where they originated on the island, but she felt confident that she could solve at least one of the mysteries of the island.

Glancing at her brother, she groaned when she saw that he had begun to play with the automatic windows in the car. Now if only she could solve the mystery of how they were related, she thought with a sigh.

Lesson 13: Fictional Portrayals of Places

Answer these questions about "The Mystery of Easter Island" and "The Island of the Statues." Write your answers in complete sentences.

1. How are the two passages similar?

_____

_____

_____

_____

2. How are the passages different?

_____

_____

_____

_____

3. Why do you think the author of "The Island of the Statues" presents a mystery to solve?

_____

_____

_____

4. How is Celine's father in the story connected to the ideas in the first passage?

_____

_____

_____

_____

Graphic Organizers

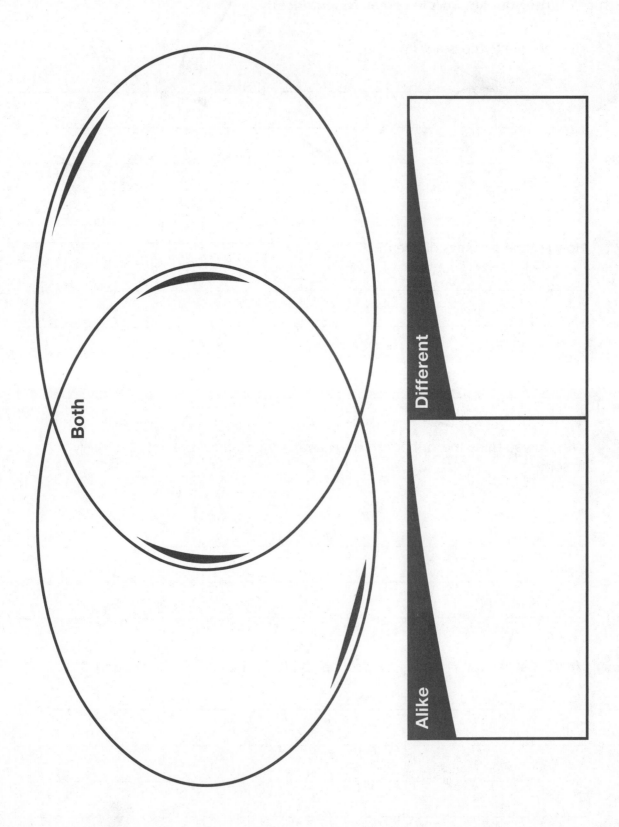

Both

Different

Alike